The Plant Cycle

by Nina Morgan

Illustrations by John Yates

Thomson Learning • New York

Books in the series

The Human Cycle
The Food Cycle
The Plant Cycle
The Water Cycle

Words printed in **bold** can be found in the glossary on page 30.

First published in the
United States in 1993 by
Thomson Learning
115 Fifth Avenue
New York, NY 10003

First published in 1993 by
Wayland (Publishers) Ltd.

Cataloging-in-Publication Data applied for

ISBN: 1-56847-091-6

Printed in Italy

Contents

A day in the life of a plant

Just as people do, plants need food, water, and air to live and grow. You cannot see plants getting bigger from minute to minute, but they are always growing. Every day they drink water through their roots, breathe, and make food in order to grow strong and healthy.

This series of photographs shows how much this daffodil has grown in only one week.

Green plants need plenty of sunshine to make their food.

Most green plants make their own food inside their leaves. To do this they need certain **ingredients**, the way a baker needs flour, sugar, and eggs to make a cake. The ingredients a plant needs to make food are sunlight, water, good soil, and air.

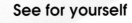

See for yourself

See for yourself how important sunlight is to plants. Plants move toward sunlight, because they need it to grow.

1. Put a small plant, such as a tomato plant, on a sunny windowsill. Don't forget to water it.
2. Watch what happens to the plant. By the end of the first week you will see how the plant has bent toward the light.
3. Turn the plant around so that it bends into the room. What happens during the next week?

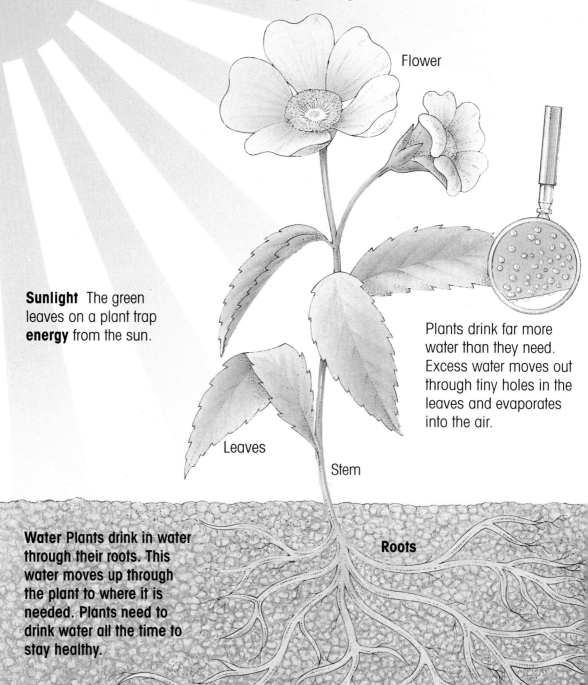

SUN

How does a plant get ingredients to make food?

Flower

Sunlight The green leaves on a plant trap **energy** from the sun.

Plants drink far more water than they need. Excess water moves out through tiny holes in the leaves and evaporates into the air.

Leaves

Stem

Water Plants drink in water through their roots. This water moves up through the plant to where it is needed. Plants need to drink water all the time to stay healthy.

Roots

Air We breathe in air through our nostrils. A plant takes in air through tiny holes in its leaves. The plant uses some parts of this air to make food. It breathes out the rest as waste.

If you put a bunch of flowers in a glass vase, you can see how much water they drink. The water level drops after a few days.

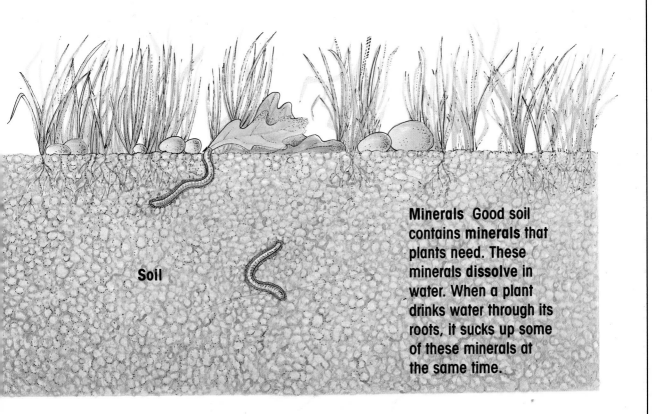

Soil

Minerals Good soil contains **minerals** that plants need. These minerals **dissolve** in water. When a plant drinks water through its roots, it sucks up some of these minerals at the same time.

See for yourself

Plants drink in far more water than they need. This water travels up through the plant to where it is needed. When the water reaches the leaves, it move out through tiny holes, called pores, and **evaporates** into the air.

1. Water a small plant thoroughly.
2. Place a clear plastic bag over the plant in the evening.
3. Secure the bottom of the bag with a rubber band.
4 In the morning, you will find water on the inside of the plastic bag.

The reproduction cycle

Different plants live for different amounts of time. Some trees, such as the giant sequoia, pictured here, live for many hundreds of years. One giant sequoia tree in California is about 2,500 years old. Flowering garden plants often live for only a few months.

A family of plants can live for much longer than a single plant. That is because, like people, plants **reproduce**. There are many special ways that they can do this. Sometimes only one plant is needed. Spider plants produce new plants from parts of their roots, shoots, or leaves. Other plants, such as irises, can grow a whole new plant from just a tiny piece of root. The new plant will be exactly like the parent it grew from.

See for yourself

Some plants can reproduce from just part of a root. The carrots we eat are actually the roots of the carrot plant.

1. Cut off a piece of carrot near its top.
2. Place this piece in a saucer with a little bit of water.

After a few days you will see shoots growing from the top.
What is the plant doing?

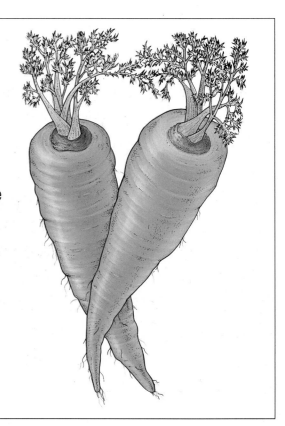

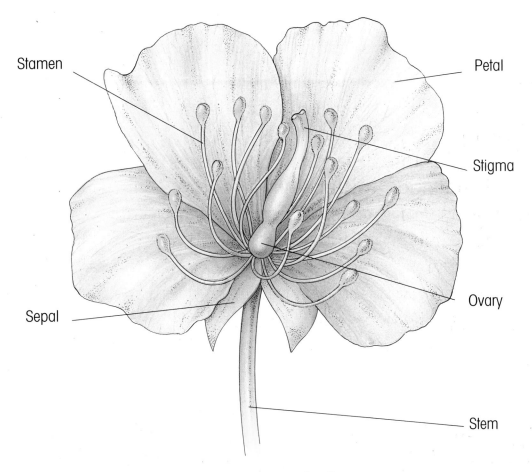

Stamen

Petal

Stigma

Sepal

Ovary

Stem

A typical flower head, with the main reproductive organs of a flower shown.

Sometimes two plants are needed. **Pollen** from one plant joins with egg **cells** from another plant to make seeds. This is called **fertilization**.

Pollen and egg cells are found inside the flowers of a plant. Sometimes, if you carefully tap a flower over your palm, a fine dust will fall out. This is the pollen falling off the stamens. The egg cells are found inside the **ovary**. You can see the ovary and stamens in the picture on this page.

When the wind blows, the seeds in a dandelion clock are carried on the breeze.

colored flowers or sweet **nectar** to attract insects, such as bees. Pollen sticks to the insects, who then carry it to the other flowers.

Before a new plant can grow, the seeds must land on good soil. Plants spread their seeds in many ways. Some seeds are blown by the wind and some float on the water. Others are eaten by animals and left in the animals' droppings, far from the parent plants.

There are different ways for pollen and egg cells from two plants to meet. Usually the pollen has to reach the egg cell. Some plants produce huge clouds of pollen that are blown around by the wind, until some pollen comes to rest on another plant. Others have brightly

Some seeds are eaten by animals.

When the time is right, the seeds will **germinate**, or begin to grow. When they mature, they will reproduce, as their parents did.

...and finally the leaves.

...then the shoot...

First the root...

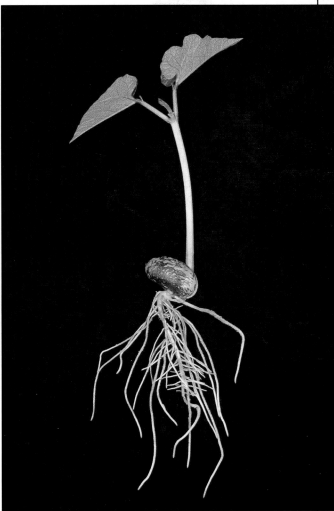

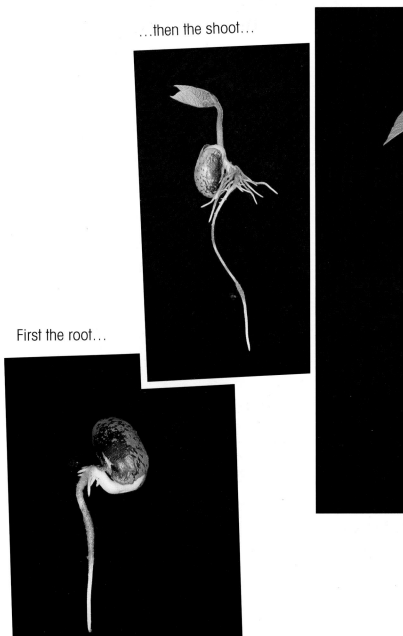

These pictures, from left to right, show what happens when a seed germinates.

Seasonal cycles

In spring many plants grow new shoots and leaves. New plants grow, too. Trees that lose their leaves in the fall grow leaves again.

Throughout summer different plants flower and reproduce. Some make seeds from which new plants will grow.

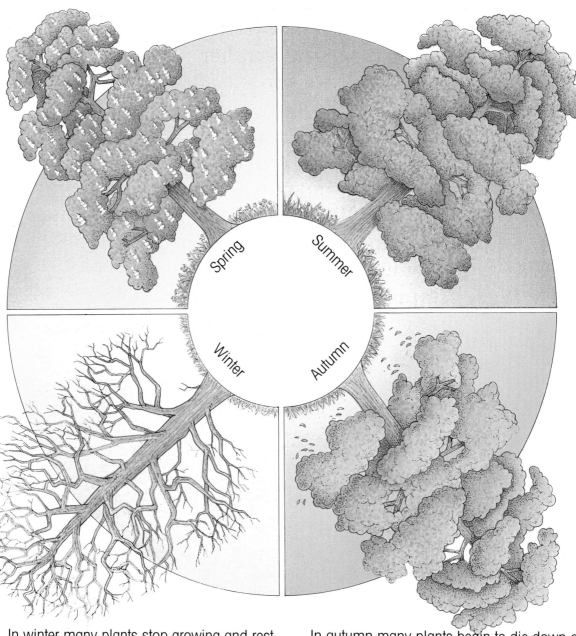

Spring

Summer

Winter

Autumn

In winter many plants stop growing and rest during the cold, dark, short days and long nights. Other die. Some trees have no leaves.

In autumn many plants begin to die down or rest. The leaves on some trees change color and fall to the ground.

In winter people wear warm clothes, eat hot food, and stay indoors when it is too cold outside. In summer people wear cool clothing and spend lots of time outside. Some stay up later at night. Plants change with the seasons, too. The different weather tells plants when to rest, grow, reproduce, and die.

In winter, when it is cold and dark, most plants rest. Instead of making new food, they live on food they made and stored earlier in the year, when there was more sunshine. Some plants wither every winter. They look as if they have disappeared or are dead. In spring they quickly begin to grow new shoots and leaves.

Winter brings cold, dark, short days, and perhaps snow. These changes affect all living things, including people.

In winter temperatures drop and the ground may freeze. Plants stop growing and some die.

Deciduous trees lose their leaves every winter and grow new ones in the spring.

Evergreens are trees that lose their leaves throughout the year, but because they are always growing new leaves they never look bare. In spring the days get longer and the ground warms up. There is more sunlight, so plants come to life.

In spring the sun's rays warm the soil again. This encourages plants to grow and trees to sprout leaves and blossom.

When daylight lasts for the right number of hours a plant will blossom. It gently unfolds its petals to the sunlight. These three photographs show a poppy flower unfolding its petals.

They begin to make more food. Many plants use the energy they get from this food to grow new shoots. Deciduous trees start to grow new leaves.

In summer the days become even longer and hotter. These changes make different plants act in different ways. Some plants will only flower and reproduce when daylight lasts for many hours. Others will reproduce earlier in the season. Each plant will flower at its own special time and leave behind seeds. These will grow into new plants the next year.

When autumn approaches the days begin to grow cooler and shorter again. Deciduous trees begin to lose their leaves and other plants begin to rest. Some plants die.

In winter a lot of plants stop growing. They rest through the cold, short, dark winter days. They will continue their life cycle in spring, when the ground warms up and the days get longer.

These changes—which take place in spring, summer, autumn, and winter—are called seasonal cycles.

In the center of this poppy are stamens. They are covered with pollen. Pollen is needed to fertilize the egg cells.

Life after death

Certain things happen to a piece of fruit when it is thrown away. It begins to turn brown. It becomes smelly and soft. It might grow a furry covering called mold. Finally, it shrivels up and disappears. In short, it rots or **decays**.

The furry covering on these strawberries is mold. It rots the fruit.

This also happens to plants when they die. Old pieces of fruit or dead plants may look completely lifeless. In fact they are seething with millions of tiny living creatures called **bacteria**. Although we cannot see them, bacteria are in the air and on surfaces all around us. They feed on dead plants and animals and make them decay.

This fungus is growing on a dead tree stump. Like bacteria, fungus grows on dead material and makes it rot.

Have you ever seen toadstools or mushrooms in the woods? They grow on dead plants, trees, and animals. They are **fungi**. Like bacteria, fungi feed and grow on dead material and make it rot.

When a plant or tree decays, it becomes smaller and eventually seems to disappear. This is because it is broken into tiny bits by the bacteria and fungi. These bits go back into the soil. The minerals the plant used when it was alive go back into the soil, too.

Dead leaves and wood eventually rot back into the soil. The goodness they return to the soil is used by new shoots to help them grow.

Soon this goodness is taken up and used by new, growing plants. In this way, dead plants help new plants grow strong and healthy.

See for yourself

The bacteria and fungi that rot plants work more quickly in warm places.

1. Cut a piece of fruit in two pieces.
2. Put one piece in the refrigerator, and leave the second piece in a warm place.

Which piece shows the first signs of the tiny threads of fungi or mold? Which piece decays faster?

Always changing

Plants, like people, are not all the same. On a tiny patch of ground there are usually many different types of plants. Each type has its own special needs. Some like sunny spots, others like shade. Some grow best in the shelter of other plants. Some like a certain type of soil. When lots of different plants live together, it is called a plant **community**.

These beautiful flowers are growing in a desert, where there is very little rain. Some other plants would find it very difficult to grow here.

Some plants find exactly what they need on a certain patch of land and grow very well. They become strong and healthy and make lots of new plants. Other plants are not as lucky. They do not find everything they need to grow.

These four diagrams explain how succession works. The diagram below shows three plants—A, B, and C—growing on the same patch of ground.

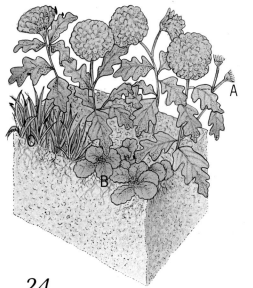

Plant A finds the minerals it needs in the soil. It grows tall and strong, becoming the strongest plant.

Usually these plants can still grow, but they will be weaker and produce fewer new plants.

As the strong plants grow, they change the ground around them. Perhaps they are very tall plants and so make it shady. Perhaps they drink up a lot of water and make the ground dry. These changes can make the ground ideal for other plants, which also begin to grow well. Soon they become the strongest. This cycle of change is known as **succession**.

Succession also happens as the seasons change. Some plants grow best in winter, others in spring or summer. As the weather changes with the seasons, different plants become the strongest. Plant communities are always changing.

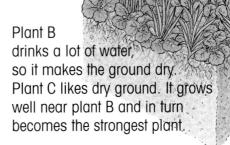

As plant A grows tall, it makes the ground shady. Plant B likes shade. It grows strong and healthy in the shade of plant A and soon becomes the strongest plant.

Plant B drinks a lot of water, so it makes the ground dry. Plant C likes dry ground. It grows well near plant B and in turn becomes the strongest plant.

Breaking the cycle

Whenever you dig up a patch of ground to make a garden, you are destroying a natural plant community. This is not always a bad thing to do, because gardens can be very beautiful, interesting, restful, and pleasing.

Many plants survive in gardens because people work hard to make things right for them. For example, they pull out weeds so that the garden plants do not have to fight with the weeds for sunlight and **nutrients** in the soil. Weeds are not bad plants. They are just plants that are growing where some people do not want them.

People also destroy plant communities when they grow food. If farmers want to grow wheat, for example, they have to make sure that the wheat plants have everything they need.

Gardeners spend a lot of time pulling up weeds so that flowers can grow strong and healthy.

Some weeds, like this bindweed, can be very beautiful.

To start with, the farmer needs a field. He or she may have to plow a meadow or clear a forest where many different types of plants and animals live. If the farmer already has a field, he or she will have to get rid of many other plants in the field, including any weeds. Farmers may also want to add minerals to the soil to make it richer. **Insecticides** might be sprayed on the wheat to kill insects and to help the crops grow.

This farmer is plowing a field. When a farmer gets a field ready to plant a crop, he or she has to get rid of any plants and weeds already growing there.

Many farmers set fire to rain forests. They want to clear the ground to use it for farming.

In Brazil some people have cleared huge areas in the **tropical rain forests** to grow crops or to provide grazing land for animals. They argue that the wood from the trees can be sold to bring in money to the area, and that the land is needed to grow food.

Other people argue that the rain forests are too precious to destroy.

Over thousands of years, they have become the home of millions of different plants and animals. Many of them are not found anywhere else.

No one knows all the details of how the rain forests work, or whether the rain forest will come back if it is destroyed. But is is clear that when people change the balance of nature, it is important to consider carefully what might happen.

See for yourself

Crops grow best when they do not have to fight with other types of plants.

1. Clear two patches of ground.
2. In both patches plant several rows of radish seeds. Keep both plots well watered.
3. Carefully keep one patch free of weeds (be careful not to pull out radish plants by mistake). Leave the other plot alone.
4. Wait for three or four weeks.

Which patch grows the largest number of plant species? Which plot grows the best radishes? (If you want to do this experiment inside, plant you radish seeds in deep trays of soil. Add grass seed to one of the trays.)

Glossary

Bacteria Very small living things that are all around us. They can be seen with a microscope. Some make living things decay.

Community A group of plants and animals that live together in the same area an affect each other's lives.

Decay To rot.

Deciduous Trees that lose their leaves in autumn.

Dissolve To melt into something. Salt dissolves in water.

Egg cells Tiny parts of a plant found in the ovary. They mix with pollen to make seeds.

Energy Something living things need to move, grow, and breathe. Plants and animals cannot live without energy.

Evaporate To turn into water vapor (like steam from a teakettle) or gas.

Evergreens Trees that lose and grow leaves all year round. They never look bare.

Fertilization The joining of male and female cells to form a seed.

Fungi Plants that do not make their own food. They live on rotting plants and animals.

Germinate To sprout; to begin to grow.

Ingredients Things that go into a mixture.

Insecticides Chemicals used to protect plants from insects and diseases. Many of them are poisonous.

Minerals Substances found in the earth. Many are needed by plants to grow strong and healthy.

Nectar A sweet liquid found in some flowers.

Nutrients All the things that a plant or other living thing needs to remain healthy.

Ovary The part of a plant where egg cells are produced and kept.

Pollen A powder in flowers that joins with egg cells to make new seeds.

Reproduce To produce offspring.

Succession When new and different plants and animals thrive in an area as conditions change.

Tropical rain forests Thick forests with high rainfall that are found near the equator. They are full of many thousands of types of plants and animals.

Further reading

Challand, Helen. *Plants Without Seeds*. Plants. Chicago: Childrens Press, 1986.

Ganeri, Anita. *Plants*. Nature Detective. New York: Franklin Watts, 1992.

Jordan, Helene J. *Seeds by Wind and Water*. New York: Harper Collins, 1962.

Madgwick, Wendy. *Flowering Plants*. The Green World. Austin: Steck- Vaughn, 1990.

Stidworthy, John. *Plants and Seeds*. Through the Microscope.
   New York: Gloucester, 1990.

Taylor, Barbara. *Green Thumbs Up! The Science of Growing Plants*.
   New York: Random House, 1992.

Picture acknowledgments
The publishers would like to thank the following for allowing their photographs to be reproduced in this book: Bruce Coleman (cover picture, center), 4 (J. Burton), 5 (Dr. E. Potts), 7 (E. Craddock), 12 (both, J. Burton), 13 (all, K. Taylor), 15 (bottom, J. Shaw), 16 (Dr. S. Nielsen), 17 (F. Prenzel), 21 (K. Taylor), 24 (top, M. P. Price, bottom, H. Reinhard); Geoscience Features 26 (bottom); Science Photo Library 18-19 (all C. Nuridsany & M. Perennou), 20 (Dr. J. Burgess), 28 (Dr. M. Read), Planet Earth 22 (H. C. Heap); Tony Stone Worldwide (cover picture, background), 15 (top, L. Adamski Peek), 27 (A. Sacks), Zefa 23, 26 (top).

Index

DATE DUE			

581
MOR

Morgan, Nina.

The plant cycle

SUTTON ELEMENTARY LIBRARY
HOUSTON TX 77074